HOMO SAPIENS - I

A COMPILATION OF EPIC POETRY ABOUT THE ELEMENTS THAT DEFINE HUMANITY

MAWPHNIANG NAPOLEON

This book is a collection of personal thoughts and research of the author.

It is a product of the author's own perspective and understanding of the world.

The author apologizes if this book offends anyone, as it is not intended to do so.

The intention of this book is to provoke thought, ponder and to support and inspire readers.

The author has chosen to focus on various random elements and topics that make us human, specifically, the 'Homo Sapiens'. This book is the first in a series of books that the author plans to write on this topic.

The author would like to express his sincere gratitude to his parents, Mrs Shiba Mawphniang and Late Mr Wesly Roy Pomshong, who taught him the value of love and support.

The author would also like to express his gratitude to his partner, Miss Clarissa Candace Giri Khyriemujat, Bah Rangdajied Marwein, Dada John Gomar-MZ, and his siblings, Emi Kwisdora, James H, Martin L, Baiahun, Baiasuk, Baiakmen Mawphniang, who have always been there for him.

The author also wants to express his gratitude to his friends and family for their goodness, and for helping him understand more about human relationships.

Lastly, the author would like to express his gratitude to the ups and downs and the fate of life in grand scheme of things, for helping him grow and understand more about himselfs and the world.

Thank you.

Khublei shihajar Nguh

Dhanewad

Contents

Foreword

"Welcome to 'Homo Sapiens: A Compilation of Epic Poetry about the Elements that Define Humanity.' This book is the first installment in a series that explores the complexities of what it means to be human through the powerful medium of poetry.

Inside, you'll find a diverse collection of poems that delve into various aspects of humanity, from the beauty of music and the power of love, to the trials of mistakes and the raw emotions of grief and loss. The poems also explore the relationship of humanity with nature and the elements, such as ash, rain, cloud, and fire.

This book is a celebration of the human experience in all its complexity and nuance. It is a reminder that we are all connected by our shared humanity, and that the beauty and pain of our existence is what makes us truly alive.

We hope that this book will inspire you to reflect on your own experiences and to find meaning and beauty in the world around you. It is a gift to be shared and discussed, to be read and re-read, to be felt and remembered.

So, sit back, relax, and let the words of this book transport you on a journey through the elements that define us as Homo Sapiens. We hope you enjoy the ride."

Preface

"Welcome to the first installment of the Homo Sapiens series, 'A Compilation of Epic Poetry About the Elements that Define Humanity.' This book is a collection of poems that delve into the depths of what it means to be human. Each poem explores a different aspect of humanity, from the beauty of love to the power of music, the pain of mistakes to the wonder of nature.

In this book, you will find poems on a diverse range of topics such as Homo Sapien, Poetry, Music, Mistake, Love, Ash, Rain, Cloud, and Fire. Each poem offers a unique perspective on the human experience, providing a window into the hearts and minds of those who wrote them.

As you read through this collection, we hope that you will find something that resonates with you, something that makes you feel seen and understood. We also hope that it will inspire you to explore your own humanity and the humanity of those around you.

This is just the first part of the series and expect more exciting topics to come in the next installment. Thank you for joining us on this journey of self-discovery through poetry.

Happy reading!"

Acknowledgements

"I am deeply grateful to the many individuals who have supported me in the creation of this book. My heartfelt thanks go out to my family and friends for their unwavering encouragement and love throughout this journey. I would also like to express my gratitude to my editor for their invaluable guidance and expertise in helping to shape the manuscript. Lastly, I would like to thank all of the literary figures whose works have influenced and inspired me throughout my life."

Prologue

"Welcome to this thought-provoking book that delves into the various topics that define humanity. As you read through its pages, you will encounter a wide range of ideas and perspectives that will challenge your understanding of what it means to be human.

This book is not meant to provide definitive answers, but rather to provoke thought and encourage further exploration. We encourage you to take a pen and paper and make note of any points that you feel need more detail in the next edition. Your thoughts and insights are valuable to us, and we want to ensure that this book is as thought-provoking and informative as possible.

Throughout the book, we will explore different aspects of humanity, from the nature of love and the power of music to the pain of mistakes and the wonder of nature. We hope that you will find something that resonates with you, something that makes you feel seen and understood.

As you read, we encourage you to keep an open mind and be willing to consider different perspectives. We believe that true understanding comes from a willingness to engage with different ideas, even if they challenge our own beliefs.

We hope that this book will inspire you to explore your own humanity and the humanity of those around you. So, take a seat, open your mind, and dive into the pages of this thought-provoking journey.

Happy reading!"

MAWPHNIANG NAPOLEON

HOMO SAPIENS - I

A COMPILATION OF EPIC
POETRY ABOUT THE
ELEMENTS THAT DEFINE
HUMANITY.

With grateful heart, I offer up this book,

A product of my mind and endless toil,

And thank you, dear reader, for your look,

Your interest and your time, a precious spoil.

I hope within its pages you will find

A wealth of knowledge, joy, and inspiration,

A guide to life, a window to the mind,

A spark to light the fire of your imagination.

But should you find a flaw or want for more,

Please do not hesitate to send me word,

For I am always eager to explore

New ways to make this book more than preferred.

So thank you, dear reader, for your support,

Your feedback will help make this book more short.

Mawphniang Napoleon

Syadheh, Ri Bhoi District - 793105

Meghalaya, India malung3@gmail.com.

This book is a collection of personal thoughts and research of the author.

It is a product of the author's own perspective and understanding of the world.

The author apologizes if this book offends anyone, as it is not intended to do so.

The intention of this book is to provoke thought, ponder and to support and inspire readers.

The author has chosen to focus on various random elements and topics that make us human, specifically, the 'Homo Sapiens'. This book is the first in a series of books that the author plans to write on this topic.

1. Reflections of a Wise Man: The Paradox of Homo Sapiens

Verily, Homo sapiens, the wise man, a creature of earth

Endowed with reason and intellect, of great worth

A product of evolution, of natural selection

A species apart, with unique reflection

But what is it that sets us apart?

Is it our ability to reason, to think and to chart

The mysteries of the universe, the secrets of life

Or is it our capacity for love, for joy and for strife

We have built great civilizations, created art and science

Conquered nature, and found ways to coexist in compliance

But with our intellect, comes the burden of choice

And the question of purpose, in this vast universe without voice

Are we but mere accidents, in the grand scheme of things

Or is there a higher purpose, for which our existence brings

These are questions that have puzzled man for ages

And yet, despite our knowledge, the answers still eludes and rages

But perhaps, the true measure of our worth

Is not in the answers we find, but in the questions we birth

For it is in our quest for understanding

That we continue to evolve, and in the end, stand tall and commanding

So let us embrace our humanity, with all its flaws and grace

And strive to reach for the stars, in this infinite space

For in our quest for knowledge, we are truly Homo sapiens

The wise man, forever seeking, forever transcending.

But as we reach for the stars and unlock the secrets of the universe,

We must not forget our humble origins, and the earth that gave us birth.

For we are but mere mortals, bound by the laws of physics and biology
And as we continue to evolve, we must tread lightly, and not become lost in
our own hubris.
We have the power to shape the world, to shape our destiny
But with that power comes responsibility, to preserve and not destroy, to live
in harmony.
For we are but one species, among many on this planet
And it is our duty to protect and respect all forms of life, for they too have a
right to exist.
But as we strive to improve and evolve, let us not forget our humanity
For it is our emotions, our empathy and our compassion, that makes us truly
human.
Let us not become cold and calculating, in our pursuit of progress
For it is in our humanity, that we find our truest success.
So let us continue to evolve and reach for the stars, but always remember
That we are Homo sapiens, the wise man, and our humanity is what makes us
forever a wonder.
As we journey on this path of evolution and progress,
We must not forget the fragility of our existence, and the transience of our
success.
For all that we have achieved, all that we have built,
Will one day crumble and fade, and our legacy be spilt.
But in the face of this mortality, let us not despair
For though our time on this earth is fleeting and rare,
We have the power to make a difference, to leave our mark
To make the world a better place, and to leave a legacy that will spark.
Let us strive to be the best version of ourselves,
To be kind, to be compassionate and to be true.
Let us not waste our time in the pursuits of superficiality,
But rather strive to make a meaningful contribution to humanity.
So let us embrace our humanity, with all its flaws and grace

And strive to reach for the stars, in this infinite space

For in our quest for knowledge and progress, we are truly Homo sapiens

The wise man, forever seeking, forever transcending, and forever living on.

As we continue to evolve, we must not forget our past,

For it is the foundation upon which our future is cast.

We must learn from the mistakes of our ancestors,

And strive to make a better world, free from the shackles of hate and rancor.

We have the power to shape the world, to shape our destiny

But with that power comes responsibility, to preserve and not destroy, to live in harmony.

For we are but one species, among many on this planet,

And it is our duty to protect and respect all forms of life, for they too have a right to exist.

We must also strive to understand our place in the universe,

To comprehend the vastness of space, and the enormity of time.

We must not be content with our limited understanding,

But continue to seek truth, and to unravel the mysteries that still bind.

We are Homo sapiens, the wise man, a creature of earth

Endowed with reason and intellect, of great worth

But our true worth is not in the answers we find,

But in the questions we birth and how we use our mind.

So let us continue to evolve, to seek, and to wonder,

For it is in this journey, that we truly flourish and thunder.

But as we reach for the stars, and unlock the secrets of the universe,

We must not forget our place in the grand scheme of things,

For we are but a small part of a greater cosmic tapestry,

And our actions have consequences that ripple far beyond our earthly being.

We must strive to live in harmony with the natural world,

And respect the delicate balance that sustains life.

We must learn to live sustainably, and not exploit the earth,

For it is the only home we have, and it is our ultimate worth.

We must also strive to understand the diversity of life,

And appreciate the beauty and wonder that surrounds us.

For we are but one part of the great web of life,

And our fate is intricately linked with that of all other living things.

We are Homo sapiens, the wise man, a creature of earth,

Endowed with reason and intellect, of great worth.

But our true worth is not in the answers we find,

But in how we use our wisdom, to live in harmony and peace with all mankind.

So let us continue to evolve, to seek, and to wonder,

But let us also strive to live in harmony with the world, and to make it a better place for all under.

As we continue to evolve, we must also strive to understand the complexities of our own minds.

For though we possess great intellect and reason,

We are also subject to the whims of emotion and passion.

We must learn to harness our inner selves,

To control our impulses and to act with reason.

For the true measure of wisdom, is not only in knowledge,

But in the ability to use it, to make the world a better place and live in accordance.

We must also strive to understand the diversity of human experience,

To appreciate the richness of cultures and perspectives.

For though we may differ in our beliefs and ways of life,

We are all connected by our shared humanity, and our ultimate goal should be to strive for peace and strive.

We are Homo sapiens, the wise man, a creature of earth,

Endowed with reason and intellect, of great worth.

But our true worth is not in the answers we find,

But in how we use our wisdom, to live in harmony with ourselves, others, and the world combined.

So let us continue to evolve, to seek, to wonder and to strive,

For it is in this journey, that we truly live, and our purpose truly derive.

As we evolve, we must also remember that the journey of progress is not
without its struggles and setbacks.

For every step forward, there may be a step back.

But it is through these challenges that we grow, and learn to adapt and
overcome.

We must not let setbacks and failures discourage us,

But instead, use them as opportunities to learn and improve.

For progress is not a linear path, but a winding road,

And it is through perseverance and determination that we will find a way to
go.

We must also remember that progress is not just about material advancement,

But also about moral and ethical growth.

We must strive to be better people, not just for ourselves, but for others,

And to leave a positive impact on the world, for future generations to discover.

We are Homo sapiens, the wise man, a creature of earth,

Endowed with reason and intellect, of great worth.

But our true worth is not in the answers we find,

But in how we use our wisdom, to better ourselves, and to make a better
world, that is refined.

So let us continue to evolve, to seek, to wonder, to strive and to overcome,

For it is in this journey, that we truly live, and our purpose is truly won.

As we continue to evolve, we must also remember that we are not alone in this
journey.

We are a part of a larger community, a part of a greater human race.

And it is through cooperation and collaboration, that we will be able to
achieve more, and reach greater heights of progress.

We must strive to build bridges, not walls,

And to work together, despite our differences and falls.

For it is through unity, that we will be able to overcome the challenges that we face,

And to build a better world, in a much more sustainable pace.

We must also remember that progress is not just about us,

But also about the well-being of future generations, and the earth that we trust.

We must ensure that our actions are sustainable,

And that we leave behind a world that is healthy, and just.

We are Homo sapiens, the wise man, a creature of earth,

Endowed with reason and intellect, of great worth.

But our true worth is not in the answers we find,

But in how we use our wisdom, to build a better world, for all of mankind.

So let us continue to evolve, to seek, to wonder, to strive, to overcome and to cooperate,

For it is in this journey, that we truly live, and our purpose truly elevate.

As we continue to evolve, we must also remember that the journey is not just about achieving material or scientific advancements but also about our own personal growth. It's about becoming the best version of ourselves, to be kind, compassionate and true.

We must strive to be humble and honest, to be empathetic and understanding,

To be willing to listen, to learn and to grow, both in our knowledge and in our being.

We must also strive to be responsible for our own happiness and well-being,

And to find a sense of purpose and meaning in our lives, to overcome our own suffering.

We are Homo sapiens, the wise man, a creature of earth,

Endowed with reason and intellect, of great worth.

But our true worth is not in the answers we find,

But in how we use our wisdom, to live a good life, that is kind.

So let us continue to evolve, to seek, to wonder, to strive, to overcome, to
cooperate, and to reflect,
For it is in this journey, that we truly live, and our purpose truly connect.
As we continue to evolve, we must also remember that our journey is not just
about ourselves, but also about the impact that we have on others and the
world around us. We must strive to make a positive difference, to help others,
and to leave the world a better place than when we found it.
We must strive to be selfless and generous, to be compassionate and
understanding,
To use our wisdom, not just for our own benefit but for the betterment of
humanity and the world.
We must also strive to be responsible citizens, to be aware of the world around
us, to be informed and to act with a sense of civic duty. To contribute to the
betterment of society and the welfare of mankind.
We are Homo sapiens, the wise man, a creature of earth,
Endowed with reason and intellect, of great worth.
But our true worth is not in the answers we find,
But in how we use our wisdom, to make a positive impact, that is kind.
So let us continue to evolve, to seek, to wonder, to strive, to overcome, to
cooperate, to reflect and to serve,
For it is in this journey, that we truly live, and our purpose truly preserve.
As we continue to evolve, we must also recognize that our journey is not just
about reaching a destination, but about the journey itself. It is about the
experiences we have, the people we meet, and the memories we create along
the way.
We must strive to live in the present, to be mindful and aware of the world
around us,
To appreciate the beauty of life, and to make the most of every moment we
have.
We must also strive to be open to new experiences, to be curious and
adventurous,

To be willing to take risks and to try new things, to grow and to evolve.

We are Homo sapiens, the wise man, a creature of earth,

Endowed with reason and intellect, of great worth.

But our true worth is not in the answers we find,

But in how we use our wisdom, to live a fulfilling life, that is kind.

So let us continue to evolve, to seek, to wonder, to strive, to overcome, to cooperate, to reflect, to serve and to appreciate,

For it is in this journey, that we truly live, and our purpose truly shape.

As we continue to evolve, we must also remember that our journey is not just about reaching a destination but about the impact that we have on the world and on future generations. We must strive to leave behind a legacy that is positive, meaningful and enduring.

We must strive to be remembered for our kindness, our generosity, and our compassion,

And for the positive impact that we have had on the world and on others.

We must also strive to make a difference, to leave the world a better place than when we found it,

And to inspire future generations to continue the journey of progress, enlightenment, and evolution.

We are Homo sapiens, the wise man, a creature of earth,

Endowed with reason and intellect, of great worth.

But our true worth is not in the answers we find,

But in how we use our wisdom, to leave a legacy that is kind.

So let us continue to evolve, to seek, to wonder, to strive, to overcome, to cooperate, to reflect, to serve, to appreciate and to leave a legacy,

For it is in this journey, that we truly live, and our purpose truly be.

As we continue to evolve, we must also remember that our journey is not just about achieving success but also about the importance of humility and the ability to learn from our mistakes. We must strive to be open-minded and humble, to acknowledge when we are wrong and to be willing to learn from our mistakes.

We must strive to be resilient and adaptable, to be able to bounce back from adversity and to learn from our failures.

We must also strive to be humble in our successes, to acknowledge that our achievements are not solely due to our own efforts but also the contributions of others, and the opportunities and circumstances that were presented to us.

We are Homo sapiens, the wise man, a creature of earth,

Endowed with reason and intellect, of great worth.

But our true worth is not in the answers we find,

But in how we use our wisdom, to be humble, and to learn from our mistakes and to grow forth.

So let us continue to evolve, to seek, to wonder, to strive, to overcome, to cooperate, to reflect, to serve, to appreciate, to leave a legacy and to be humble,

For it is in this journey, that we truly live, and our purpose truly humble.

As we continue to evolve, we must also remember that our journey is not just about individual success but also the collective well-being of humanity and the planet. We must strive to be responsible global citizens and to work towards the greater good of all.

We must strive to be inclusive and equitable, to advocate for the marginalized and the underprivileged, and to work towards a more just and fair society.

We must also strive to be environmentally conscious and to work towards preserving the planet for future generations.

We are Homo sapiens, the wise man, a creature of earth,

Endowed with reason and intellect, of great worth.

But our true worth is not in the answers we find,

But in how we use our wisdom, to work towards the greater good and to leave a positive impact on the world.

So let us continue to evolve, to seek, to wonder, to strive, to overcome, to cooperate, to reflect, to serve, to appreciate, to leave a legacy, to be humble and to work towards the greater good,

For it is in this journey, that we truly live, and our purpose truly understood.

As we continue to evolve, we must also remember that our journey is not just about accumulating knowledge, but also about the wisdom to apply it in meaningful ways. We must strive to use our knowledge to make a positive impact on the world and to help others.

We must strive to be critical thinkers and to question the status quo, to challenge our own beliefs, and to seek truth and understanding.

We must also strive to be responsible creators, to use our knowledge and skills to innovate and improve the world, but also to consider the potential consequences and implications of our actions.

We are Homo sapiens, the wise man, a creature of earth,

Endowed with reason and intellect, of great worth.

But our true worth is not in the answers we find,

But in how we use our wisdom, to apply our knowledge and to make a positive impact that is kind.

So let us continue to evolve, to seek, to wonder, to strive, to overcome, to cooperate, to reflect, to serve, to appreciate, to leave a legacy, to be humble, to work towards the greater good and to apply our knowledge in meaningful ways,

For it is in this journey, that we truly live, and our purpose truly pays.

As we continue to evolve, we must also remember that our journey is not just about acquiring power and material possessions, but also about inner strength and inner peace. We must strive to find balance and harmony within ourselves, to control our desires and to lead a peaceful and contented life.

We must strive to be self-aware and self-reflective, to understand our own thoughts and emotions, and to strive for inner growth and self-improvement.

We must also strive to be non-judgmental and accepting of others, to be understanding and empathetic, and to strive for peaceful and harmonious relationships with others.

We are Homo sapiens, the wise man, a creature of earth,

Endowed with reason and intellect, of great worth.

But our true worth is not in the answers we find,

But in how we use our wisdom, to find inner peace, and to lead a harmonious life that is kind.

So let us continue to evolve, to seek, to wonder, to strive, to overcome, to cooperate, to reflect, to serve, to appreciate, to leave a legacy, to be humble, to work towards the greater good, to apply our knowledge in meaningful ways, and to find inner peace,

For it is in this journey, that we truly live, and our purpose truly be at ease.

As we continue to evolve, we must also remember that our journey is not just about achieving our own personal goals and aspirations, but also about the impact that we have on others and the world around us. We must strive to make a positive difference in the lives of others, to help and support those in need, and to leave the world a better place than when we found it.

We must strive to be selfless, to put the needs of others before our own, and to use our talents and resources to make a difference in the world.

We must also strive to be compassionate and understanding, to be willing to listen and to learn from others, and to work towards creating a more just and equitable society.

We are Homo sapiens, the wise man, a creature of earth,

Endowed with reason and intellect, of great worth.

But our true worth is not in the answers we find,

But in how we use our wisdom, to make a positive impact on the lives of others, and to leave the world a better place that is kind.

So let us continue to evolve, to seek, to wonder, to strive, to overcome, to cooperate, to reflect, to serve, to appreciate, to leave a legacy, to be humble, to work towards the greater good, to apply our knowledge in meaningful ways, to find inner peace, and to make a positive impact on the lives of others,

For it is in this journey, that we truly live, and our purpose truly serve.

As we continue to evolve, we must also remember that our journey is not just about the present but also about the future. We must strive to think about the long-term impact of our actions and decisions, and to plan for a sustainable future for ourselves and for future generations.

We must strive to be forward-thinking, to anticipate future trends and challenges, and to work towards creating a better future for all.

We must also strive to be responsible stewards of the earth, to preserve the planet's resources and biodiversity, and to work towards a sustainable future for all living things.

We are Homo sapiens, the wise man, a creature of earth,

Endowed with reason and intellect, of great worth.

But our true worth is not in the answers we find,

But in how we use our wisdom, to think about the future and to create a sustainable future that is kind.

So let us continue to evolve, to seek, to wonder, to strive, to overcome, to cooperate, to reflect, to serve, to appreciate, to leave a legacy, to be humble, to work towards the greater good, to apply our knowledge in meaningful ways, to find inner peace, to make a positive impact on the lives of others, and to think about the future,

For it is in this journey, that we truly live, and our purpose truly conserve.

As we continue to evolve, we must also remember that our journey is not just about individual achievements but also about the collective progress of humanity. We must strive to work together, to share our knowledge and resources, and to collaborate towards a common goal of improving the human condition.

We must strive to be open-minded and inclusive, to appreciate diversity and to work together, despite our differences.

We must also strive to be visionary, to look beyond the present, and to work towards a future that is better for all mankind.

We are Homo sapiens, the wise man, a creature of earth,

Endowed with reason and intellect, of great worth.

But our true worth is not in the answers we find,

But in how we use our wisdom, to work together, to achieve collective progress and to create a better future for all mankind.

So let us continue to evolve, to seek, to wonder, to strive, to overcome, to cooperate, to reflect, to serve, to appreciate, to leave a legacy, to be humble, to work towards the greater good, to apply our knowledge in meaningful ways, to find inner peace, to make a positive impact on the lives of others, to think about the future, and to work together,

For it is in this journey, that we truly live, and our purpose truly unite.

As we continue to evolve, we must also remember that our journey is not just about material advancements, but also about spiritual growth. We must strive to understand our place in the world, to connect with something greater than ourselves, and to find meaning and purpose in our lives.

We must strive to be open-minded, to explore different spiritual practices, and to find what resonates with us.

We must also strive to be compassionate and understanding, to respect the spiritual beliefs of others and to foster a sense of unity and interconnectedness.

We are Homo sapiens, the wise man, a creature of earth,

Endowed with reason and intellect, of great worth.

But our true worth is not in the answers we find,

But in how we use our wisdom, to connect with something greater than ourselves, to find meaning and purpose in our lives and to create a sense of interconnectedness and unity.

So let us continue to evolve, to seek, to wonder, to strive, to overcome, to cooperate, to reflect, to serve, to appreciate, to leave a legacy, to be humble, to work towards the greater good, to apply our knowledge in meaningful ways, to find inner peace, to make a positive impact on the lives of others, to think about the future, to work together, and to find spiritual growth,

For it is in this journey, that we truly live, and our purpose truly be fulfilled.

As we continue to evolve, we must also remember that our journey is not just about the present, but also about the past and the future. We must strive to learn from the past, to understand its lessons and to use them to shape a better future.

We must strive to be curious and open-minded, to explore and understand the history of our species, cultures, and civilizations.

We must also strive to be respectful and mindful, to acknowledge the mistakes and injustices of the past and to work towards creating a more equitable and just future.

We are Homo sapiens, the wise man, a creature of earth,

Endowed with reason and intellect, of great worth.

But our true worth is not in the answers we find,

But in how we use our wisdom, to learn from the past, to understand its lessons and to shape a better future.

So let us continue to evolve, to seek, to wonder, to strive, to overcome, to cooperate, to reflect, to serve, to appreciate, to leave a legacy, to be humble, to work towards the greater good, to apply our knowledge in meaningful ways, to find inner peace, to make a positive impact on the lives of others, to think about the future, to work together, to find spiritual growth, and to learn from the past,

For it is in this journey, that we truly live, and our purpose truly be, in the past, present and future.

2. Poetry: A Timeless Art

Verse and rhyme, a timeless art,

A form of expression, from the heart.

A medium for the musings of the mind,

A way to leave the world of the blind.

Poetry, a tool for the bard,

To weave tales of love, life, and regard.

A language of the soul, a voice of the spirit,

A way to make meaning, without fail or merit.

With each stanza, a new thought unfolds,

A journey through emotions, stories told.

From the depths of despair, to the heights of elation,

Poetry captures it all, in its purest sensation.

The pen, a sword, the paper, a shield,

A way to fight the battles of the field.

To speak truth, to challenge the status quo,

To inspire change, and to make the world grow.

But poetry is not just for the grandiose,

It's for the simple, the mundane, and the prosaic.

For in the smallest moments, lies the greatest beauty,

And poetry, a way to capture and make it our duty.

So let us raise our pens, and write,

For in poetry, the world takes flight.

A canvas for the human experience,

A way to make sense, of the chaos and the fence.

So here's to poetry, the eternal muse,

A form of art, that will never refuse,

To take us on a journey, of the heart and the mind,

A way to leave the world of the blind, behind.
And yet, despite its power and grace,
Poetry remains a mystery in many a place.
For some, it's but a trifle, a thing of the past,
For others, a puzzle, that forever will last.
But in its complexity, lies its simplicity,
For poetry, is but the reflection of humanity.
It's the voice of the oppressed, the song of the free,
A mirror to our souls, and all we wish to be.
It's the whisper of the wind, and the roar of the sea,
A symphony of words, that sets the spirit free.
It's the poetry of nature, and the poetry of man,
A language that unites us, and helps us to understand.
For poetry is not just about rhyme and verse,
It's about the human condition, and the universe.
It's about our struggles, and our triumphs, too,
It's about the mystery of life, and what we can do.
So let us continue to explore this art,
And let poetry, forever, hold a special part
In our hearts, and in our minds, as we journey on,
For in poetry, we find, a way to be strong.
And as we delve deeper into the realm of verse,
We come to realize the true power and purpose,
Of poetry, as a means of self-expression,
And a way to connect with others, and form a connection.
It's a way to explore the depths of the human mind,
And to examine the complexities of the human kind.
A tool for introspection, and for contemplation,
A way to make sense of the world, and our relation.
For poetry is not just about the words on the page,
But about the emotions and experiences, they engage.

It's about the feelings, it evokes, and the thoughts it inspires,
And the way it touches us, on a deeper level, entire.
So let us continue to celebrate this art,
And let poetry, forever, play a vital part
In our lives, as we seek to understand,
The beauty and mystery, of the world, and of man.
For in poetry, we find meaning, and purpose,
A way to make sense of life, and to nurture
Our souls, and our spirits, as we journey through,
A world of wonder, and all that is true.
And as we delve deeper into the intricacies of verse,
We are reminded of the profound universality of poetry's curse,
For it is not bound by borders, or language, or time,
It is a form of expression, that will forever chime.
From ancient Greece, to modern day,
Poetry has found its way,
To the hearts and minds of people everywhere,
A universal language, that we all can share.
It is a way to bridge the gap, between cultures and nations,
And to promote understanding, and compassion.
Through the power of words, and the beauty of rhyme,
Poetry brings us together, in a world, that can seem so sublime.
And yet, it is also a reminder, of our unique individuality,
For each poet, brings their own perspective, and reality.
It is a way to explore, our own thoughts and emotions,
And to find our own voice, in a world of commotion.
So let us continue to appreciate, this art form,
And let poetry, forever, be a source of warmth
In our hearts, as we navigate the world, and our place,
For in poetry, we find the beauty, and the grace.
As we delve deeper into the world of verse,

We come to realize the depth of poetry's curse,

For it is not just about the words on the page,

But about the emotions and experiences they engage.

It is a way to explore the human condition,

And to examine the complexities of the mind and emotion.

It is a tool for self-reflection and for exploration,

A way to connect with others and form a deeper connection.

Poetry is a way to express our innermost thoughts and feelings,

And to make sense of the world and its dealings.

It is a way to give voice to the silenced and the oppressed,

And to challenge the status quo and bring about progress.

And yet, it is also a way to celebrate life and its beauty,

To find joy in the simple things and to see the world in its entirety.

Poetry is a reminder that in the midst of chaos, there is still art,

And in the darkest moments, there is still a light that guides us to the heart.

So let us continue to appreciate this art form,

And let poetry forever be a source of warmth.

For in poetry, we find meaning, and purpose,

And a way to navigate the world with grace and confidence.

As we delve deeper into the realm of poetry,

We come to see the power of its versatility.

For it is not just about rhyme and meter,

But about the message and the feelings it generates.

Poetry is a way to explore the human experience,

And to give voice to the emotions that are often left in silence.

It is a way to convey meaning, and to make sense of the world,

And to connect with others in a way that is profound and unfurled.

It is not just for the poets and the bards,

But for anyone who seeks to express themselves, with open hearts.

Poetry is for the young and the old, for the rich and the poor,

For anyone who wishes to explore their inner thoughts and more.

And yet, it is also a reminder that words are powerful,

And that they can shape the world, in ways both beautiful and awful.

Poetry is a call to action, and to reflection,

And to use our words, with purpose, and discretion.

So let us continue to explore this art form,

And let poetry be a constant source of warmth.

For in poetry, we find meaning, and purpose,

And a way to navigate the world, with grace and endurance.

As we delve deeper into the world of poetry,

We come to see the power of its malleability.

For it is not just a tool for expression,

But also a tool for self-discovery and introspection.

Poetry is a way to explore the depths of the human soul,

And to give voice to the thoughts and feelings that make us whole.

It is a way to understand the world and our place in it,

And to connect with others on a level that is intimate.

It is not just for the traditional poets and bards,

But for anyone who wishes to explore their creative sides and impart.

Poetry is for the young and the old, for the rich and the poor,

For anyone who wishes to tap into the beauty of language and more.

And yet, it is also a reminder that words have power,

And that they can be used to create or to devour.

Poetry is a call to action, and to reflection,

And to use our words with care, and with discretion.

So let us continue to appreciate this art form,

And let poetry forever be a source of warmth.

For in poetry, we find meaning, and purpose,

And a way to navigate the world with elegance and verve.

As we delve deeper into the realm of poetry,

We come to see the boundless possibilities it offers, free.

For it is not just a tool for self-expression,

But also a tool for social change and introspection.
Poetry is a way to give a voice to the voiceless,
And to shed light on the injustices that are often thoughtless.
It is a medium to raise awareness and to inspire action,
And to connect with others in a way that promotes compassion.
It is not just for the literary elite,
But for anyone who wishes to tap into their creative seat.
Poetry is for the young and the old, for the rich and the poor,
For anyone who wishes to express themselves, and explore.
And yet, it is also a reminder that words have power,
And that they can be used to create or to cower.
Poetry is a call to action, and to reflection,
And to use our words with care, and with discretion.
So let us continue to celebrate this art form,
And let poetry forever be a source of warmth.
For in poetry, we find meaning, and purpose,
And a way to navigate the world, with elegance and endurance.
As we delve deeper into the world of poetry,
We come to see its ability to transcend boundaries, seamlessly.
For it is not just a tool for self-expression,
But also a tool for cultural preservation and connection.
Poetry is a way to keep alive the stories and traditions,
Of our ancestors and of the diverse cultures, in positions.
It is a medium to pay homage to the past,
And to connect with our heritage, and make it last.
It is not just for the poets and the literati,
But for anyone who wishes to tap into the beauty of language and its parity.
Poetry is for the young and the old, for the rich and the poor,
For anyone who wishes to express themselves, and discover more.
And yet, it is also a reminder that words have power,
And that they can be used to unite or to cower.

Poetry is a call to action, and to reflection,

And to use our words with care, and with discretion.

So let us continue to appreciate this art form,

And let poetry forever be a source of warmth.

For in poetry, we find meaning, and purpose,

And a way to navigate the world, with elegance and cultural endurance.

As we delve deeper into the realm of poetry,

We come to see its ability to transcend time and history.

For it is not just a tool for self-expression,

But also a tool for exploring the human condition, and its progression.

Poetry is a way to explore the human experience,

And to give voice to the emotions that are often left in silence.

It is a way to convey meaning, and to make sense of the world,

And to connect with others on a level that is profound and unfurled.

It is not just for the poets and the bards,

But for anyone who seeks to express themselves, with open hearts.

Poetry is for the young and the old, for the rich and the poor,

For anyone who wishes to explore their inner thoughts, and more.

And yet, it is also a reminder that words have power,

And that they can shape the world, in ways both beautiful and sour.

Poetry is a call to action, and to reflection,

And to use our words, with purpose, and discretion.

So let us continue to explore this art form,

And let poetry be a constant source of warmth.

For in poetry, we find meaning, and purpose,

And a way to navigate the world, with grace and perseverance.

As we delve deeper into the world of poetry,

We come to see its ability to transcend the barriers of formality.

For it is not just a tool for self-expression,

But also a tool for breaking conventions and experimenting with originality.

Poetry is a way to explore new forms and styles,

And to push the boundaries of language and its miles.

It is a way to challenge the status quo, and to innovate,

And to connect with others in a way that is truly great.

It is not just for the traditional poets and bards,

But for anyone who wishes to tap into their creative sides, and depart

From the norm, and to discover new ways of expression,

And to connect with the world, in a unique session.

And yet, it is also a reminder that words have power,

And that they can be used to create or to devour.

Poetry is a call to action, and to reflection,

And to use our words with care, and with discretion.

So let us continue to appreciate this art form,

And let poetry forever be a source of warmth.

For in poetry, we find meaning, and purpose,

And a way to navigate the world, with elegance, originality and endurance.

3. Ethereal Symphony: A Musical Ode to the Mystery and Beauty of Sound

Oh music, sweet symphony of sound

A melody that can elevate one from the ground

A harmony that can soothe the mind

A rhythm that can leave one entwined

With notes and chords, a symphonic dance

An art that can give life to circumstance

A language that transcends words and speech

A universal force that can bring peace

But what is it that makes music so grand?

Is it the notes that we hear, or the feelings they command?

Is it the structure and form, or the emotions they express?

Is it the beauty of sound, or the memories they possess?

Perhaps it is all of these and more

A mystery that we can never explore

For music is a ethereal thing

A force that can make our hearts sing

It is the sound of nature and the silence of the night

A reflection of our souls and an insight

It is the rhythm of life, a symphony divine

A song that will always be forever mine

So let us listen and embrace the tune

For music is the language of the moon,

The poetry of the stars, the symphony of the sea,

A treasure that will always be.

But music is not just a mere pleasure,

It is a tool for personal treasure,

A way to express the deepest emotions,

A key to unlock the mind's notions.

It can evoke memories of the past,

Or paint a vision of a future that will last,

It can bring to light the beauty of the now,

And help us navigate life's ebbs and flows.

Music is a mirror of the human soul,

A reflection of our joys and our woes,

It has the power to heal and to mend,

A force that can transcend.

But it is not only for the individual,

It is also a social ritual,

A way to connect and to bond,

A shared experience that can transcend beyond.

So let us listen and let the music flow,

For it is a gift that we must always know,

To treasure and to nurture, to love and to share,

For music is the language of the soul, and it will always be there.

But as we bask in the beauty of music,

We must also remember its use can be misused,

For it can be a tool for manipulation,

A weapon for propaganda and exploitation.

So let us listen with a critical ear,

And question the message we hear,

For music, like all forms of art,

Can be a reflection of the human heart.

And as we listen, let us also create,

For it is in the act of creation, we truly elevate,

The power of music lies not only in its sound,

But in the way it allows us to be truly profound.
So let us sing, let us play,
Let us create, let us sway,
For music is not just a thing to be heard,
But a force to be felt, a truth to be worded.
Oh music, sweet symphony of sound,
A melody that can elevate one from the ground,
A harmony that can soothe the mind,
A rhythm that can leave one entwined.
And as we continue to create and to listen,
Let us also remember the power of music's mission,
To bring people together, to break down barriers,
To unite us in a common language, free from terrors.
For music knows no boundaries, no race, no creed,
It is a universal force that can plant a seed,
Of empathy, of understanding, of love,
A reminder that we are all stars shining above.
So let us continue to make and to hear,
To let the music wash over us and wipe away our tear,
For in this sweet symphony of sound,
We can truly be free, truly be found.
Music is the beating heart of humanity,
A source of inspiration, a guide to our destiny,
So let us honor it, let us cherish it,
For in music, we can truly transcend.
And as we continue to explore the depths of music,
Let us also remember its power in the political and socioeconomic issues,
It has been a tool for the oppressed to voice their struggle,
A way for marginalized communities to express themselves and make their
struggle visible.
For music is not only a form of entertainment,

But also a form of resistance, a call for change,

It has the power to inspire, to mobilize, to create a movement,

A call to action for a better future, a call to redemption.

So let us not just listen to music passively,

But actively engage with its message, its meaning, its plea,

For music is not just a form of art,

But a tool for activism, a call to the heart.

As we continue to appreciate the beauty of music,

Let us also remember its power to bring about change and to heal,

For in music, we can find solace, hope, and the power to make a difference,

A reminder that we are all capable of creating a better existence.

And as we continue to delve deeper into the world of music,

Let us also remember its ability to evoke different emotions,

It can be melancholic, joyful, nostalgic, melancholic, soothing, or invigorating,

A reflection of the human experience and its complexities.

Music is a powerful medium that can take us on a journey,

It can transport us to different times and places,

It can remind us of our past, and inspire our future,

It can make us laugh, cry, and feel alive.

As we continue to listen and create,

Let us also remember the importance of preserving and sharing,

For music is a legacy, a heritage, and a tradition,

That should be passed down to future generations, to continue to enrich their lives.

So let us continue to sing, play and dance,

To let the music fill our hearts, and enhance,

Our lives, our souls, and our world,

For music is the universal language that can bring us together and make us whole.

And as we continue to immerse ourselves in the world of music,

Let us also remember its role in shaping our culture,

It has the power to influence fashion, art, and literature,

To reflect society's values, beliefs and aspirations.

Music is a reflection of the times,

It captures the spirit of the era,

It tells the story of the people,

And shapes the way we see the world.

As we continue to enjoy the beauty of music,

Let us also acknowledge its role in shaping our identity,

For music is not just a form of entertainment,

But a fundamental aspect of who we are as individuals and as a society.

So let us continue to explore, to create and to appreciate,

The power of music and its ability to transform and elevate,

Our lives, our culture and our world,

For in music, we can find meaning, purpose, and a sense of belonging,
unfurled.

And as we continue to delve deeper into the world of music,

Let us also remember its ability to transcend time and space,

The music that we listen today, can have the same emotion it had centuries
ago,

It can connect us to our ancestors and to our cultural heritage.

Music has the power to bring people together,

To bridge gaps, to unite, and to create a sense of unity,

It can transcend all barriers, be it language, culture or religion,

And remind us that we are all part of the same human community.

As we continue to listen and create,

Let us also remember the importance of innovation and experimentation,

For music is an ever-evolving art form,

That needs to be constantly pushed, challenged and transformed.

So let us continue to appreciate the beauty of music,

In all its forms, and let us always strive to discover new musical horizons,

For music is not just a form of entertainment,
But a powerful force that can shape our lives and our world, and that should always be cherished and honored.
And as we continue to embrace the world of music,
Let us also remember its ability to evoke personal memories and experiences.
Music has the power to transport us back in time, to specific moments in our lives,
Bringing back emotions, feelings and sensations that are deeply personal.
Music can be a powerful trigger for memories,
It can help us remember the past, to process emotions, and to make sense of our experiences.
As we continue to listen and create,
let us also remember the importance of music in our personal growth and self-discovery,
For music has the ability to help us connect with ourselves, to find meaning and purpose,
and to help us navigate the journey of life.
So let us continue to cherish and honor the beauty and power of music,
In all its forms, and let us always strive to discover new musical horizons,
For music is not just a form of entertainment,
But a powerful force that can shape our lives, our world and our self, and that should be always cherished and honored.
And as we continue to delve deeper into the world of music,
Let us also remember its impact on our mental and physical well-being.
Music has the power to reduce stress, anxiety and depression,
It has also been found to have positive effects on pain management, sleep, and overall health.
Music therapy is a well-established practice in many hospitals, rehabilitation centers, and mental health clinics,
It is used to promote healing, alleviate symptoms, and improve quality of life.
As we continue to listen and create,

let us also remember the importance of music in our overall well-being,

For it has the power to heal, to soothe, and to improve our lives.

So let us continue to cherish and honor the beauty and power of music,

In all its forms, and let us always strive to discover new musical horizons,

For music is not just a form of entertainment,

But a powerful force that can shape our lives, our world, our self, and our

well-being, and that should be always cherished and honored.

And as we continue to explore the world of music,

Let us also remember its role in education and personal development.

Music education has been shown to have a positive impact on cognitive

development,

It can improve memory, concentration, and problem-solving skills.

It also helps to develop fine motor skills, coordination, and discipline,

Music education can also foster creativity, self-expression, and a love of

learning.

As we continue to listen and create,

let us also remember the importance of music education,

For it has the power to enhance personal development and open doors to new

opportunities.

So let us continue to cherish and honor the beauty and power of music,

In all its forms, and let us always strive to discover new musical horizons,

For music is not just a form of entertainment,

But a powerful force that can shape our lives, our world, our self, our

well-being, and our personal development, and that should always be

cherished and honored.

And as we continue to embrace the world of music,

Let us also remember its ability to bring people together, to create

communities and to foster a sense of belonging.

Music has the power to bring people of different backgrounds, cultures, and

ages together,

It creates a common ground, a shared experience, and a sense of connection.

Music festivals, concerts, and other events,

Bring people from different walks of life together, to share in the joy and passion of music.

As we continue to listen and create,

Let us also remember the importance of music in building and strengthening communities,

For it has the power to bring people together, to foster understanding and to create a sense of belonging.

So let us continue to cherish and honor the beauty and power of music,

In all its forms, and let us always strive to discover new musical horizons,

For music is not just a form of entertainment,

But a powerful force that can shape our lives, our world, our self, our well-being, our personal development and our communities, and that should always be cherished and honored.

And as we continue to delve deeper into the world of music,

Let us also remember its role in storytelling and preserving history and culture.

Music has the ability to convey stories, myths, and legends,

It is a medium through which culture and history are passed on from generation to generation.

Music has the ability to preserve the language, customs, and traditions of a people,

It can keep alive the memory of the past and connect us to our heritage.

As we continue to listen and create,

Let us also remember the importance of music in preserving and sharing culture and history,

For it has the power to keep alive the memory of the past and connect us to our heritage.

So let us continue to cherish and honor the beauty and power of music,

In all its forms, and let us always strive to discover new musical horizons,

For music is not just a form of entertainment,

But a powerful force that can shape our lives, our world, our self, our
well-being, our personal development, our communities, and our cultural
heritage, and that should always be cherished and honored.
And as we continue to immerse ourselves in the world of music,
let us also remember its ability to inspire and bring about change.
Music has the power to inspire us to dream, to believe and to take action,
It can be a catalyst for social, political, and personal change.
From protest songs to anthems of hope and freedom,
music has played a vital role in shaping our world and our history.
As we continue to listen and create,
let us also remember the importance of music in inspiring change and
promoting progress,
For it has the power to inspire us to dream and to make a difference.
So let us continue to cherish and honor the beauty and power of music,
In all its forms, and let us always strive to discover new musical horizons,
For music is not just a form of entertainment,
But a powerful force that can shape our lives, our world, our self, our
well-being, our personal development, our communities, our cultural heritage,
and our future, and that should always be cherished and honored.

4. The Beauty of Mistakes

In the realm of human endeavor,
A notion oft-pondered, forever and ever,
Is the concept of mistake,
And the impact it doth make.
Some may view it as a curse,
A blemish on one's verse,
A misstep on life's grand stage,
A cause for eternal rage.
But others, more wise and sagacious,
Perceive it as an opportunity auspicious,
A chance for growth and self-improvement,
A means for self-exaltment.
For in the making of a mistake,
We are gifted a chance to undertake,
The task of introspection,
And gain from our own imperfection.
For what is a mistake,
But a lesson to be learned,
A step on the path to wisdom's gate,
And the opportunity to be earned.
So let us not bemoan our errors,
But rather embrace them, like true terrors,
For in the end, 'tis through our mistakes,
That our character truly awakes.
But oft-times, in our haste,
We fail to see the beauty in our waste,
And instead, we wallow in regret,

Forgetting that mistakes are not a debt.

For every misstep that we make,

Is a chance for our souls to awake,

And see the world in a new light,

With a newfound wisdom and insight.

So let us not fear the unknown,

But instead, boldly walk alone,

For in the end, 'tis through our mistakes,

That we find the path to true greatness.

For mistakes are not a hindrance,

But a path to true transcendence,

A stepping stone on the journey of life,

A means to reach our true strife.

So let us not dwell on the past,

But instead, look forward and steadfast,

For in the end, 'tis through our mistakes,

That we find the true meaning of grace.

So let us embrace our mistakes,

And let them be the fire that fuels our fate,

For in the end, 'tis through our mistakes,

That we rise victorious and truly great.

But it is not just through our own mistakes,

That we learn and grow, to our own sakes,

For in the mistakes of others, we also find,

A reflection of ourselves, and a new state of mind.

For in the faults of others, we see,

Our own potential to be free,

From the shackles of our own imperfection,

And find true liberation and connection.

So let us not judge or cast blame,

For in doing so, we only taint our own name,

But instead, let us strive to understand,
And offer a helping hand.
For in the end, it is through empathy,
That we find true humility,
And in understanding the mistakes of others,
We find a path to true brotherhood and sisters.
So let us not fear the mistake,
But embrace it, for its true worth to make,
For in the end, 'tis through our mistakes,
That we find true growth, and the path to awake.
But let us not forget,
That mistakes, while they may be a debt,
To be paid with lessons learned and growth,
They can also cause great harm and loss.
For some mistakes, though well-intentioned,
Can lead to pain and destruction,
And it is then, that true remorse,
Must be felt, and actions must enforce.
For to make amends, to repair the damage done,
Is the only way, to regain what's lost, to be won,
And to move forward, with a newfound humility,
And a vow, to not repeat the same malady.
So let us not view mistakes,
As mere opportunities, to be embraced,
But also, as a call to action,
To make things right, with compassion.
For in the end, 'tis through our mistakes,
That we find true growth and awakeness,
But also, it is through owning up to our errors,
That we find true redemption and success.
And as we journey through life's twists and turns,

Let us not forget the lessons learned,
From the mistakes we've made along the way,
For they have shaped us, in a unique way.
For some mistakes, though hard to bear,
Have taught us strength, and how to care,
For others, and for ourselves, with grace,
And have helped us find our place.
And some mistakes, though they may seem small,
Have led to moments, that changed it all,
And have shown us, that in life's uncertainty,
There is beauty, in its variety.
So let us not view mistakes, as a curse,
But rather, as a part of life's verse,
For they have led us, to where we stand,
And have helped us, understand.
That in the end, it's not the mistakes we make,
But how we learn from them, and how we take,
The lessons learned, and use them well,
To live a life, that's true, and excel.
And as we journey through life's winding path,
Let us not forget the aftermath,
Of the mistakes we've made, and the pain they've caused,
For they have left a mark, that cannot be paused.
For the mistakes we make, have ripple effects,
That can impact the lives of those we've affected,
And it is our duty, to make things right,
And bring back the light.
For true growth, and true redemption,
Comes not just from self-reflection,
But also, from taking responsibility,
For the impact of our actions, on society.

So let us not shy away,
From the mistakes we make each day,
But rather, let us face them head on,
And work towards atonement.
For in the end, it's not the mistakes we make,
But how we learn from them, and how we take,
The lessons learned, and use them well,
To make the world a better place, and excel.
And as we go through life's journey,
Let us not forget, that mistakes are not a burden, but a plenty.
They are a reminder that we are alive,
And that there is more to learn and strive.
For every mistake, is a chance to grow,
To let go of our ego, and be more humble and low.
It's a chance to be kinder, and more compassionate,
And to build stronger relationships.
For every mistake, is a chance to learn,
To let go of our judgment, and be more concerned.
It's a chance to be more forgiving, and more understanding,
And to build a more inclusive and loving world.
So let us not fear mistakes, but welcome them,
For they are not a curse, but a benediction,
That helps us grow, and become the best version of ourselves,
And to leave behind a legacy of love and wealth.
For in the end, it's not the mistakes we make,
But how we learn from them, and how we take,
The lessons learned, and use them well,
To become the person we're meant to be, and excel.

5. Stepping Stones to Progress: A Poem on the Value of Mistakes in Science

In the realm of science, a mistake doth oft occur,

For even the most brilliant mind, doth sometimes falter.

Yet it is through these errors, that progress is made,

For in the quest for knowledge, mistakes are but a stepping stone to be trodden.

The very act of experimentation, is an exercise in uncertainty,

A process of trial and error, where hypotheses are tested and disproven.

And in the face of failure, one must not despair,

For it is through persistence and perseverance, that greatness is achieved.

For every mistake, there is a lesson to be gleaned,

A newfound understanding, that was previously unseen.

And as we continue to explore the mysteries of the universe,

Let us not fear mistakes, but embrace them as opportunities to learn and improve.

So let us not be daunted by the prospect of error,

But instead, let us embrace the challenge with vigor.

For in the grand scheme of things, mistakes are but a small price to pay,

In the pursuit of knowledge, and the betterment of humanity.

And as we delve deeper into the unknown,

And unravel the secrets of the cosmos,

We must remember that even the greatest minds,

Are not immune to the occasional misstep.

But it is through these mistakes, that we evolve and grow,

And it is through our willingness to learn from them,

That we transcend our limitations, and achieve the impossible.

For it is not the absence of mistakes,

But the ability to overcome them,

That truly defines us as scientists,

And as human beings.

So let us not be afraid of making mistakes,

But instead, let us embrace them,

As the valuable tools that they are,

In the pursuit of scientific understanding,

And the betterment of humanity.

For in the end, it is not the mistakes we make,

But the lessons we learn from them,

That will be remembered in the annals of history,

As we continue to push the boundaries of knowledge and progress.

And as we embark on this journey of discovery,

Let us not forget the importance of humility,

For even the greatest minds have much to learn,

And it is only through humility that we can truly grow.

For in the face of our mistakes,

We must not cling to our pride,

But instead, we must be open to learning,

From our peers and those who have gone before us.

And as we learn from our mistakes,

Let us not forget to share our knowledge,

With those who come after us,

For it is through the sharing of knowledge,

That we can truly make a difference.

So let us embrace our mistakes,

As opportunities for growth and learning,

And let us share our knowledge,

With the world, for the betterment of all.

And as we continue to explore the vast expanse of the universe,

Let us not forget the importance of collaboration,

For it is through the collective efforts of many,

That we can achieve greater progress.

For in the field of science, there are no lone geniuses,

But instead, a community of minds working together,

To unravel the mysteries of the world,

And make new discoveries that benefit us all.

And as we work together,

Let us not forget to be open-minded,

For it is through openness and diversity,

That we can bring new perspectives,

And achieve breakthroughs that we never thought possible.

So let us embrace our mistakes,

As opportunities for growth and learning,

Let us share our knowledge,

And work together, for the betterment of all.

For it is through our mistakes, that we learn,

And it is through our collective efforts, that we excel.

And as we continue our quest for knowledge,

Let us not forget the importance of ethics,

For it is through responsible and ethical research,

That we can ensure that our discoveries are used for the betterment of
humanity.

For science is not just about making new discoveries,

But also about using them to improve the lives of people,

And it is through ethical considerations,

That we can ensure that our research causes no harm.

And as we make new breakthroughs,

Let us not forget to consider the impact of our discoveries,

On society and the environment,

And strive to make them accessible to all.

So let us embrace our mistakes,

As opportunities for growth and learning,

Let us share our knowledge,

Work together, and consider the ethics of our research,

For the betterment of all.

For it is through responsible and ethical science,

That we can truly make a positive impact on the world.

And as we strive for greatness, let us not forget that the pursuit of knowledge is a never-ending journey, and it is through our mistakes that we learn, grow and make progress.

6. Love in the Realm of Science

'Twas in the realm of science, where logic and reason reign,

That the truth of love's great power did oft reveal itself again and again.

Through every trial and tribulation, through every chemical reaction,

The beauty of love's bond, a constant satisfaction.

But alas, in the face of progress and advancement,

Love's tenets oft fell by the wayside, in a state of abandonment.

For in the quest for knowledge, the heart's desires oft ignored,

Leaving the soul in a state of emptiness, forever deplored.

Thus, I implore thee, oh scientist of great renown,

To never lose sight of love, and to always wear love's crown.

For though the mind may lead us to the stars above,

'Tis love that guides us to a life of joy and true love.

Let us not forget the power of love's chemical allure,

For it is the foundation upon which strong relationships endure.

And in the face of all the data and facts that we may collect,

Remember that love is the greatest force, and in love, we should always reflect.

So let us preach love always, in every lab and every station,

For in the end, it is love that brings true elation.

And though we may unlock the secrets of the universe,

Without love, our lives would be nothing but a curse.

So let us sing love's praises, and let our hearts be filled with cheer,

For in the realm of science, love is always near. And let us never forget that love is the most powerful force in the universe, it conquers all, and make us all better, let us all to love we must immerse.

And let us not forget that love is not limited to just romantic relationships,

But encompasses all forms of connection, be it with family, friends, or even our fellow kin.

For love is the thread that binds us all together,
Giving us the strength to weather any kind of weather.
And as we delve deeper into the mysteries of the mind,
Let us not forget the power of love to heal and bind.
For in the depths of our hearts, love is the light that guides us through,
Giving us the courage to pursue our dreams and aspirations anew.
So let us embrace love in all its forms, with open arms,
And let it be the guiding force behind all of our endeavors and calm.
For in the end, it is love that will bring us true understanding,
And lead us to a life of true flourishing and expanding.
So let us continue to preach love always, in all that we do,
For it is the one thing that will bring our world a brighter hue.
For love is the greatest force of all, it is the one that make us all.
And let us never forget that love is not limited by time or space,
But transcends all boundaries, and can bring about true grace.
For love knows no bounds, and can conquer even the greatest of fears,
And bring us to a place of unity and understanding, wiping away all tears.
And as we continue to explore the vast expanse of the universe,
Let us remember that love is the one thing that gives our lives purpose.
For it is through love that we find true meaning and fulfillment,
And it is love that brings us all together, in a bond that is truly thrilling.
So let us continue to preach love always, in all that we say and do,
For it is the one thing that will bring about true progress and breakthrough.
For in the end, love is the one thing that truly matters,
And it is through love that we will find the true meaning of life and its patterns.
And let us not forget that love is not just a feeling, but an action,
A choice we make to be kind, compassionate, and to act with satisfaction.
For love is not just about receiving, but also about giving,
It is about making sacrifices and letting go of living.
And as we continue to explore the world around us,
Let us remember that love is the one thing that gives our lives a plus.

For it is through love that we find true connection and empathy,

And it is love that brings about true change, in ourselves and in society.

So let us continue to preach love always, in all that we see and hear,

For it is the one thing that can bring about true peace and cheer.

For in the end, love is the one thing that truly sets us free,

And it is through love that we can truly be who we want to be.

Thus, let us sing love's praises, and let our hearts be filled with grace,

For in the realm of science and life, love is the one thing that will always take

its place. Love is the one thing that make us all better, let us all to love we must

immerse.

And let us not forget that love is not just about the present,

But also about the future and the legacy that we leave as a testament.

For love is about creating a better world for those who will come after,

And about leaving behind a legacy of kindness, compassion, and love that will

last forever.

And as we continue to explore the mysteries of the universe,

Let us remember that love is the one thing that gives our lives purpose.

For it is through love that we find true meaning and fulfillment,

And it is love that brings us all together in a bond that is truly thrilling.

So let us continue to preach love always, in all that we say and do,

For it is the one thing that will bring about true progress and breakthrough.

For in the end, love is the one thing that truly matters,

And it is through love that we will find the true meaning of life and its patterns.

Let us be a beacon of love and spread it everywhere,

For it is love that will bring about true harmony and repair.

Love is the answer, the solution, the key,

Let us all love and live in unity.

And let us not forget that love is not only about the self,

But also about the collective, and the well-being of everyone else.

For love is about striving for the greater good,

And about working together to make the world a better hood.

And as we continue to push the boundaries of science and technology,
Let us remember that love is the one thing that gives our lives serenity.
For it is through love that we find true connection and empathy,
And it is love that brings about true change, in ourselves and in society.
So let us continue to preach love always, in all that we see and hear,
For it is the one thing that can bring about true peace and cheer.
For in the end, love is the one thing that truly sets us free,
And it is through love that we can truly be who we want to be.
Let us spread love, like a wildfire, let it ignite,
For it is love that will bring about true unity and might.
And let us not forget that love is not only about the positive emotions,
But also about the hard work and commitment that it often demands.
For love is about working through challenges and conflicts,
And about growing and learning from the experience, and it all makes sense.
And as we continue to unlock the secrets of the universe,
Let us remember that love is the one thing that gives our lives purpose.
For it is through love that we find true meaning and fulfillment,
And it is love that brings us all together in a bond that is truly thrilling.
So let us continue to preach love always, in all that we say and do,
For it is the one thing that will bring about true progress and breakthrough.
For in the end, love is the one thing that truly matters,
And it is through love that we will find the true meaning of life and its patterns.
Let us be a shining example of love and compassion,
For it is love that will bring about true understanding and liberation.
And let us not forget that love is not only about receiving,
But also about giving and sharing, and truly believing.
For love is about selflessly caring for others,
And about making sacrifices for the greater good, like sisters and brothers.
And as we continue to explore the depths of the human mind,
Let us remember that love is the one thing that gives our lives a bind.
For it is through love that we find true connection and empathy,

And it is love that brings about true change, in ourselves and in society.

So let us continue to preach love always, in all that we see and hear,

For it is the one thing that can bring about true peace and cheer.

For in the end, love is the one thing that truly sets us free,

And it is through love that we can truly be who we want to be.

Let us be ambassadors of love and spread it far and wide,

For it is love that will bring about true unity and pride.

Love is the one thing that make us all better, let us all to love we must immerse.

Love is the only way to a harmonious and peaceful universe.

On Love II

But love is not just a matter of the heart,

It also has a scientific start.

Research shows that love can impact our health,

Lowering stress levels, and boosting our wealth.

It's been found that those who are loved and love,

Have a stronger immune system, and live longer.

Love is a powerful antidote to the above,

And should be celebrated in song and in songster.

Love is not just a feeling, but a force,

That can change the course of human history.

It has the power to unite, not to divorce,

And bring about a better world for all, surely.

So let us preach love, and let it be known,

That love is the key to a better tomorrow.

Let us all strive to make love our own,

And let it guide us in all that we borrow.

So let us embrace love, in all its forms,

And let it guide us towards a brighter dawn.

For when love reigns, all other problems will be gone,

And peace and prosperity will forever be drawn.

But love is not just a one-way street,

It requires effort and a willing heart.
It's not just about receiving, but also to meet,
The needs of the other and play your part.
True love is selfless and sacrificial,
It puts the needs of others before your own.
It's about being there through thick and thin,
And making a commitment that's fully grown.
Love is not a feeling that comes and goes,
It's a choice that we make every single day.
It's about putting in the time and the prose,
To make the relationship strong in every way.
Love is not just a word, but a verb,
It requires action and not just a thought.
It's about putting in the work, and the nerve,
To make sure the relationship is not for naught.
So let us preach love, in all its depth,
And let it be the guiding light in our path.
Let us make sure that it's the foundation and the heft,
Of all the relationships that we have.
Love is not just for the young and free,
It's for all ages and all walks of life.
It's not just for the perfect, but also for the blemished,
It's for all those who seek to find a life.
Love can be found in the most unlikely places,
It can flourish in the darkest of hours.
It's not just about the happy and the graces,
But also about the struggles and the powers.
Love is not just about the good times,
But also about being there through the bad.
It's about standing by each other's sides,
And being a partner through the happy and the sad.

Love is not just about the present,
But also about building a future together.
It's about growing old and being content,
And having a love that will last forever.
So let us preach love, in all its fullness,
And let it be the guiding star in our quest.
Let us make sure that it's the heart's completeness,
And the key to a life that's truly zest.
Love is not just for the human kind,
But also for all living beings that share the earth.
It's not just about being one of a kind,
But also about showing compassion and worth.
Love is not just about the physical touch,
But also about the mental and spiritual connection.
It's not just about the present, but also the future much,
It's about building a bond that is unbreakable and unshakable.
Love is not just a feeling, but also a state of being,
It's about creating a sense of belonging and security.
It's not just about the pleasure, but also the healing,
It's about creating a sense of completeness and purity.
Love is not just about the words, but also about the actions,
It's about showing the other person that they are valued and worthy.
It's not just about the grand gestures, but also about the small interactions,
It's about showing the other person that they are loved and cherished truly.
So let us preach love, in all its forms,
And let it be the guiding principle in all that we do.
Let us make sure that it's the driving force,
And the key to a life that is fulfilling and true.
Love is not just about the present,
But also about the past and the future.
It's not just about the good and the pleasant,

But also about the bad and the torture.
Love is not just about the easy,
But also about the hard and the challenging.
It's not just about the happy,
But also about the sad and the grieving.
Love is not just about the individual,
But also about the collective and the community.
It's not just about the self,
But also about the others and their needs.
Love is not just about the romantic,
But also about the platonic and the familial.
It's not just about the passion,
But also about the companionship and the loyal.
So let us preach love, in all its diversity,
And let it be the guiding principle in all our relationships.
Let us make sure that it's the foundation of our society,
And the key to a world that is peaceful and blissful.
Love is not just about the words we speak,
But also about the actions we undertake.
It's not just about the promises we make,
But also about the commitment we undertake.
Love is not just about the happiness we feel,
But also about the sacrifice we make.
It's not just about the ideals we appeal,
But also about the reality we undertake.
Love is not just about the perfection we seek,
But also about the imperfections we accept.
It's not just about the joys we seek,
But also about the sorrows we accept.
Love is not just about the now,
But also about the forevermore.

It's not just about the here and now,

But also about the evermore.

So let us preach love, in all its complexity,

And let it be the guiding principle in all our lives.

Let us make sure that it's the foundation of our society,

And the key to a world that is full of love, joy, and thrive.

7. Ashen Skies: A Sight of Renewal and Regret

Ashen skies, a sight most dire,

A warning of a raging fire,

A blaze that spreads with fervent might,

And leaves in its wake, a world of blight.

The ash that falls, a somber hue,

A reminder of what once grew,

A symbol of destruction's reign,

And nature's power to cause pain.

But from the ash, new life may rise,

A phoenix from the ashes, surprise,

For in destruction, there is birth,

And the cycle of life goes on, forth.

The ash that falls, a fertilizing rain,

A nourishment for growth and gain,

A reminder that in death, there's life,

And in the darkest hours, there's hope to find.

So let us not despair, in times of ash,

But look beyond, and see the flash,

Of new beginnings, yet to come,

And a brighter future, yet to be won.

But ashen skies are not just a sign of renewal,

They also bear the mark of human's evil.

For in our quest for progress and gain,

We've set the forests alight, and caused much pain.

The ash that falls, a consequence of our greed,

A reminder of the damage we've seeded,

A symbol of our disregard for the land,

And nature's wrath, at our destructive hand.

But still, we must not lose all hope,

For there's still time to change, to learn and to cope,

To mend our ways and make amends,

And strive for a future that's not just an end.

So let us take heed, of the ash that falls,

A warning of the dire consequences of our calls,

A call to action, to change our ways,

And build a future, where ash is but a passing phase.

For ash may fall, but it also gives rise to new growth,

a reminder that in every end, there is a new beginning, a new hope.

And so, let us not forget the ash that falls,

For it holds within it, the secrets of nature's calls.

It speaks of the cycle of life and death,

And the constant ebb and flow of each breath.

The ash that falls, is a reminder to respect,

The delicate balance of nature, to not neglect,

For as we tend to our own needs and desires,

We must also tend to the earth and its fires.

For the ash that falls, is not just destruction,

But also a sign of reconstruction,

A sign that the earth will always prevail,

And in the end, will always unveil.

So let us honor the ash that falls,

For in its downfall, it also calls,

For us to be mindful and take a stand,

For the preservation of this beautiful land.

And so we must tread with caution,

As we navigate this earthly motion,

For the ash that falls, is a sign of our impact,

And the choices we make, will determine our fate in tact.
We must learn to live in harmony,
With the natural world, and not merely,
Extract and consume without regard,
For the ash that falls, is a clear warning card.
For the ash that falls, is not just ash,
But the remnants of our past flash,
A reminder that we must change our ways,
Or face dire consequences in our days.
Let us not forget the ash that falls,
For it holds within it, nature's calls,
A call to action, to right our wrongs,
And build a future, where ash belongs.
Let us not be blind to the ash that falls,
For it is a sign of our missteps and falls,
A reminder that we must take responsibility,
For the health and well-being of our community.
For the ash that falls, is not just a sight,
But a reflection of our actions and plight,
A reminder that we must strive for balance,
And work towards a sustainable advancement.
Let us not forget the ash that falls,
For it holds within it, nature's calls,
A call to action, to be mindful and aware,
And build a future, where ash is but a rare.
So let us take heed of the ash that falls,
And work towards a world where it no longer calls,
A world where nature and humanity coexist,
And the ash that falls, is but a distant mist.
And as the ash falls, let us not forget,
The importance of conservation and preservation, yet,

For the ash that falls, is not just a reminder,
But a call to protect, to conserve, and to be kinder.
For the ash that falls, is a sign of loss,
Of habitats, of species, of natural boss,
A reminder that we must act with care,
To protect the biodiversity out there.
For the ash that falls, is not just ash,
But the remnants of what we've failed to save,
A reminder that we must do our part,
To ensure that nature's beauty remains in our heart.
So let us take heed of the ash that falls,
And strive to make a positive change, calls,
For the preservation of our planet earth,
And to give back, what we've taken since birth.
So as the ash falls, let us not forget,
The impact that our actions have on the earth's net,
For the ash that falls, is a symbol of our actions,
And the consequences that come with our reactions.
But with awareness and action, we can make a change,
And reduce the ash fall, its destructive range,
For in the face of ash, there is still hope,
To create a better future, where ash can no longer cope.
For the ash that falls, is a reminder to act,
And to not let nature be a victim of our impact,
So let us take heed of the ash that falls,
And work towards a future, where ash is no longer calls.
And let us look beyond the ash that falls,
To see the beauty that nature calls,
A reminder that even in the darkest hours,
There is still hope, and new life, new flowers.
So let us not be defeated by the ash that falls,

But rise above it, and answer nature's calls,
For the ash that falls, is not the end,
But a new beginning, a chance to make amends.
Let us take this opportunity, to change our ways,
And pave a better future, for future days,
For the ash that falls, is a sign of our mistakes,
But also a sign of the chances we can take.
Let us work together, to protect and conserve,
And make a better world, that we all deserve,
For the ash that falls, is a reminder of our impact,
But also a reminder of the actions we can adapt.
So let us take heed of the ash that falls,
And work towards a future, where nature calls,
And the ash that falls, is but a distant memory,
In a world where balance and harmony, is the key.
As the ash falls, let us not forget,
The importance of sustainability, to not neglect,
For the ash that falls is a reminder,
Of the need to live in balance with nature, to not hinder.
Let us strive for a world where ash is rare,
Where we can live in harmony and repair,
The damage we've caused, and make amends,
For the earth and all its inhabitants, to befriend.
For the ash that falls is not just ash,
But the consequences of our actions and rash,
A reminder that we must be mindful and aware,
And take action towards a sustainable repair.
So let us take heed of the ash that falls,
And work towards a world, where nature calls,
And the ash that falls is but a distant dream,
In a world where balance and harmony, is supreme.

As the ash falls, let us not forget,

The importance of education and knowledge, to not neglect,

For the ash that falls is a reminder,

Of the need to educate, and to be kinder.

Let us strive to educate ourselves and others,

About the importance of conservation, and the dangers of burning coals,

For only with education and knowledge, can we make informed decisions,

And work towards a sustainable future, without any divisions.

For the ash that falls is not just ash,

But the results of our ignorance and rash,

A reminder that we must strive for education,

And take action towards a sustainable solution.

So let us take heed of the ash that falls,

And work towards a world, where education calls,

And the ash that falls is but a distant memory,

In a world where knowledge and understanding, is the key.

As the ash falls, let us not forget,

The importance of community, to not neglect,

For the ash that falls is a reminder,

Of the need to come together, and be kinder.

Let us strive to build and strengthen our communities,

To work together, to fight against environmental maladies,

For only with a united front, can we make a difference,

And work towards a sustainable future, with persistence.

For the ash that falls is not just ash,

But the result of a lack of community and a clash,

A reminder that we must strive for unity,

And take action towards a sustainable community.

So let us take heed of the ash that falls,

And work towards a world, where community calls,

And the ash that falls is but a distant memory,

In a world where unity and cooperation, is the key.
As the ash falls, let us not forget,
The importance of taking personal responsibility, to not neglect,
For the ash that falls is a reminder,
Of the role each individual plays, in this global finder.
Let us strive to take personal responsibility,
For our actions and their impact on the environment and society,
For only with individual accountability, can we make a change,
And work towards a sustainable future, that is not strange.
For the ash that falls is not just ash,
But the result of lack of personal responsibility, a clash,
A reminder that we must take ownership,
And take action towards a sustainable future, with no downturn.
So let us take heed of the ash that falls,
And work towards a world, where personal responsibility calls,
And the ash that falls is but a distant memory,
In a world where individual actions align with sustainability.
As the ash falls, let us not forget,
The importance of innovation, to not neglect,
For the ash that falls is a reminder,
Of the need to find new solutions, that are kinder.
Let us strive to be innovative,
In our approach to conservation and sustainability,
For only with new technologies and ideas, can we make progress,
And work towards a sustainable future, that is flawless.
For the ash that falls is not just ash,
But the result of a lack of innovation, a harsh clash,
A reminder that we must be forward-thinking,
And take action towards a sustainable future, with no shrinking.
So let us take heed of the ash that falls,
And work towards a world, where innovation calls,

And the ash that falls is but a distant memory,

In a world where new ideas align with sustainability.

As the ash falls, let us not forget,

The importance of resilience, to not neglect,

For the ash that falls is a reminder,

Of the need to adapt and overcome, to be kinder.

Let us strive to be resilient,

In the face of environmental challenges and adversity,

For only with the ability to adapt and overcome, can we survive,

And work towards a sustainable future, that will thrive.

For the ash that falls is not just ash,

But a test of our resilience, a harsh gash,

A reminder that we must be strong and persistent,

And take action towards a sustainable future, with no resistance.

So let us take heed of the ash that falls,

And work towards a world, where resilience calls,

And the ash that falls is but a distant memory,

In a world where adaptability aligns with sustainability.

8. Rain's Symphony

In a world so vast and wide,
Where oceans ebb and rivers glide,
There lies a force, both strong and mild,
That shapes the earth and all that's wild.
It falls from clouds in drops so small,
And gathers strength to rise tall,
It nourishes the land and sea,
And makes the world a place to be.
A symphony of sound it makes,
As it pours down in countless flakes,
It's music to the ears of all,
Who hear its steady, soothing call.
But when it falls in rage and wrath,
It floods the fields and wrecks its path,
A tempestuous, tumultuous force,
That leaves destruction in its course.
And yet, we cannot live without,
This vital, life-giving spout,
For without rain, the world would cease,
A barren, desolate piece of peace.
So let us honor and revere,
The rain that falls, both far and near,
For it is the lifeblood of our earth,
And gives us all a second birth.
And as the rain continues to fall,
It creates a watery curtain, on which
The colors of the world are sprawled,

A canvas painted by nature's brush.
It seeps into the soil and feeds,
The roots of plants, the seeds of weeds,
It helps to grow the food we eat,
And keeps the forests strong and neat.
It's in the rain that life is found,
And all around, it spins and swirls,
It's in the rain that beauty's found,
And in the rain that life unfurls.
It's in the rain that we see,
The cycle of life, death and rebirth,
It's in the rain that we believe,
That there's always a new start.
Rain is the giver of life,
And the force that makes us thrive,
It's the rhythm of the earth,
And the song that keeps us alive.
So let us raise our voice in praise,
For the rain that falls in endless ways,
For it is the heartbeat of our world,
And the force that keeps us unfurled.
But as we sing the rain's praise,
Let us not forget its darker side,
For in its might, it brings destruction,
And often, grief and tears to bide.
It's in the rain that we see,
The power of nature's rawest form,
It's in the rain that we feel,
The fragility of human norms.
And yet, as we stand in awe,
Of the rain's destructive force,

We must remember that it's necessary,
In the balance of our world's discourse.
For the rain, though it may bring harm,
Is also the giver of new life,
It washes away the old,
And prepares the earth for new strife.
So let us not curse the rain,
But instead, learn to understand,
That though it may bring pain,
It is a vital part of our land.
For the rain is not just water,
But a force that shapes our fate,
It is the bringer of renewal,
And the creator of our state.
So let us sing the rain's praise,
With gratitude and grace,
For it is the force that sustains us,
And guides us through life's maze.
But as we sing the rain's praise,
Let us also remember,
That we too have a role to play,
In preserving its splendor.
For the rain is not just a force,
But a resource that we must share,
And as we continue to grow,
We must learn to conserve and spare.
We must learn to reduce our waste,
And curb our consumption's tide,
For the rain is a finite resource,
And one that we cannot abide to squander and slide.
We must learn to respect its power,

And work with it, not against,
For the rain is not just a force,
But a partner in our quest.
So let us sing the rain's praise,
With knowledge and with care,
For it is the force that sustains us,
And a partner we must share.
And as we journey through this world,
With the rain as our guide,
Let us remember its importance,
And keep its beauty alive.
As we continue to sing the rain's praise,
Let us also remember its global significance
It is not just a local phenomena,
But a vital component of the earth's balance.
Rain is the driving force behind the weather systems,
That shape the climate of the world,
It is the engine that drives the hydrological cycle,
And the force that makes the earth unfurled.
It is the rain that brings the water,
To the deserts and the dry lands,
It is the rain that feeds the rivers,
And the oceans where the life expands.
It is the rain that brings the life,
To the forests and the jungles,
It is the rain that makes the earth,
A place where the nature's beauty mingle.
So let us sing the rain's praise,
With a global understanding,
For it is the force that sustains us,
And the lifeblood of the earth's branding.

And as we journey through this world,

With the rain as our companion,

Let us remember its significance,

And work towards its preservation.

As we sing the rain's praise,

Let us also remember its connection to our past,

For it has been revered and revered throughout history,

As a giver of life, a bringer of abundance, a force to be respected and at last.

In ancient cultures, it was seen as a gift from the gods,

A blessing for the crops, a sign of good luck,

In the mythology of many civilizations,

Rain was considered a sacred element, an important part of their spiritual muck.

And even today, in many cultures,

Rain holds a special significance,

It is celebrated and honored,

As a force that brings life and sustenance.

So as we sing the rain's praise,

Let us not forget its historical reverence,

For it has been an important part of human culture,

And a force that has shaped our existence.

And as we journey through this world,

With the rain as our guide,

Let us remember its importance,

Not just in our present, but throughout history's tide.

9. Clouds: A Natural Wonder

The clouds that float above our heads,
An enigma wrapped in misty beds,
A canvas painted by Nature's hand,
A symphony of beauty grand.
The cumulus and stratus forms,
That dance in sky's majestic storms,
The cirrus wisp that trails behind,
A sight that never fails to bind.
But clouds are not just for our view,
They play a role in Earth's review,
For they are part of hydrological cycle,
That keeps our planet in ecological balance.
The clouds that capture water droplets,
That fall as rain and snow, and stop it,
They shade our lands from scorching sun,
And help in weather patterns to run.
But clouds can also bring destruction,
In the form of lightning and eruption,
For they can unleash their fury wild,
And leave behind a trail of devastation piled.
So let us marvel at the clouds,
And all the secrets they shroud,
For they are a part of nature's tale,
A story yet to be fully unveil.
And as we gaze upon the clouds,
We cannot help but feel astounded,
For they are ever-changing and ephemeral,

A testament to the power of natural temporal.
Their shapes, sizes, and hues,
Are a reflection of the Earth's blues,
For they are shaped by winds and air,
A dance of elements beyond compare.
But clouds are not just a natural wonder,
They have also been studied and pondered,
For scientists and meteorologists,
Have sought to understand their mysteries.
They've learned of their role in climate change,
And how they affect the global range,
For clouds can trap heat, or reflect it away,
A delicate balance that scientists today still survey.
So let us marvel at the clouds,
And all the secrets they shroud,
For they are a part of nature's tale,
A story that forever will unveil.
And as we gaze upon the clouds,
We cannot help but feel enthralled,
For they are a living, breathing thing,
A natural beauty that makes our hearts sing.
But clouds are not just a visual treat,
They hold secrets that are yet to meet,
For they may hold clues to our past,
And insights that will forever last.
Clouds can also be a sign of change,
An indicator of weather that's strange,
For they can warn of storms to come,
And alert us to take shelter, some.
But clouds are not just a warning,
They can also be a source of inspiration,

For poets, painters and writers,
Have used clouds as their muses for fighters.
So let us marvel at the clouds,
And all the secrets they shroud,
For they are a part of nature's tale,
A story that forever will unveil.
And as we gaze upon the clouds,
We cannot help but feel humbled,
For they remind us of our place,
In this vast and infinite space.
For though we may strive to conquer,
The clouds will always be an enigma,
A reminder of the power of nature,
And the mysteries that still capture.
But clouds also remind us of hope,
For they remind us that there is scope,
For change and growth, and new beginnings,
And that the beauty of life is in its winnings.
So let us marvel at the clouds,
And all the secrets they shroud,
For they are a part of nature's tale,
A story that forever will unveil.
And may we always remember,
That the clouds, though ephemeral,
Are a symbol of the beauty and power,
That surrounds us in every hour.
And let us not forget,
the clouds also hold a technological debt,
For they play an important role in the field of science,
Providing valuable data for researchers to enhance.
Cloud seeding, for instance,

Is a technique to increase precipitation,
Clouds are artificially modified
To bring about rain or snow, as desired.
Clouds also have a significant impact
In the field of energy and power,
Solar energy is harvested from the clouds
To generate electricity in a tower.
So, as we marvel at the clouds,
Let us not only see their beauty,
But also recognize their worth
In shaping our world's future and duty.
For they are not just a spectacle,
But a force to be reckoned with,
A reminder that nature is complex,
And our understanding of it, still a myth.
And as we continue to marvel at the clouds,
Let us not forget their impact on the crowds,
For they can bring life-sustaining water,
Or bring about floods and disasters' slaughter.
Climate change has affected the clouds
Their patterns and behaviors, it has endowed,
Clouds are forming differently and shifting,
Affecting the weather and ecosystems, lifting.
It is our responsibility to understand,
The role of clouds in our land,
To study and research their behavior,
And take actions to mitigate their negative flavor.
So let us marvel at the clouds,
And all the secrets they shroud,
For they are a part of nature's tale,
A story that forever will unveil.

But let us also remember,

To respect and protect them,

For they are a vital part of our world,

And their preservation should be our unfurled.

And as we stand beneath the clouds,

And look up at their ethereal shrouds,

Let us not forget the beauty they possess,

And the magic they can manifest.

For they are a reminder of the infinite,

And the boundless nature of our existence,

They remind us that there is more to life,

Than what we can see with our mortal eyes.

And as we marvel at the clouds,

Let us also remember their role in the crowds,

For they are not just a natural wonder,

But also a crucial part of our society and culture.

So let us not just admire their beauty,

But also understand their duty,

For they are an integral part of our world,

And their preservation is a task yet to unfurl.

And as we bid farewell to the clouds,

Let us remember to always look up,

For they are a constant reminder,

Of the beauty, mystery and wonder of our world.

And as we contemplate the clouds,

let us not forget the role of crowds,

in shaping the future of our planet,

and the role of clouds in it.

For as we continue to pollute and degrade,

the natural balance of our earth, we pave

the way for clouds to change,

and affect not only us but also the generations to come.

It is our responsibility to take action,

and preserve the balance of nature's faction,

To reduce carbon emissions and pollution,

and ensure a future with clean clouds and a clean solution.

So let us marvel at the clouds,

but also take action to preserve them,

For they are not just a natural wonder,

but also a crucial part of our future.

As we look up at the clouds,

let us remember to also look within,

and take responsibility for our actions,

to ensure a sustainable future for all.

As we continue to marvel at the clouds,

let us not forget the role of crowds,

in shaping not only the future of our planet,

but also the future of humanity.

For as we strive for progress and development,

we must also remember to be cognizant

of the impact of our actions on the clouds,

and the delicate balance of nature that surrounds.

We must strive for harmony,

between human advancement and ecology,

to ensure that the clouds remain,

a symbol of beauty and not a source of pain.

We must also remember to be grateful,

for the clouds and all that they provide,

from the water they bring, to the shade they cast,

they are a gift that we must strive to preserve at last.

So let us marvel at the clouds,

and remember the role they play,

in shaping our world and our future,
and let us work to protect them in every way.

10. The Dance of Fire: A Reflection on Power and Consequence

As the flames dance and the embers glow,
We are reminded of the power we know
Of fire, the element that has shaped our fate
For better or for worse, it is our mate.
The ancient Greeks believed in the hearth
As the center of the home, the source of mirth
But fire also brings destruction and pain
A force that can never be tamed.
Science tells us of the chemical reactions
That fuel the flame, the combustion actions
But what of the metaphysics of fire?
The existential questions it inspires.
Is fire a force of creation or destruction?
A symbol of progress or regression?
It warms our homes and cooks our food
But also burns down neighborhoods.
Perhaps fire is a metaphor for life
A constant struggle between the good and strife
For without the heat and the light
There would be no growth, no life to ignite.
But as we watch the fire burn
We must also learn
To harness its power, to use it well
For in the end, it is our own hell.

So let us marvel at the fire's dance
But also take heed of its circumstance
For in its beauty and its might
Lies a warning, a warning to ignite.
And as the flames consume and the ash falls,
We are left with the remnants of our calls
For fire, though it may bring rebirth,
Also leaves behind a trail of dearth.
It reminds us of the fragility of all
The balance between the rise and fall
For as we play with fire, we must be aware
Of the consequences, the damage we bear.
But fire also brings innovation and progress
A force that can spur us to success
For without the spark of an idea,
We would be forever in a state of despair.
So let us embrace the fire's power
But also learn to use it with care
For in its light, we can see a new dawn,
But in its destruction, we see what we have withdrawn.
Fire, a force of nature and of man,
A reminder of the balance we must span
For in its beauty and its destruction
Lies a lesson, a call to instruction.
So let us be mindful of the fire we ignite,
For it is the key to our future and our plight.
For in its light, we can see the path to our salvation,
But in its destruction, we see the result of our damnation.
And as the fire burns and the smoke clears,
We are left to ponder on our fears
For fire, though it may bring warmth and light,

Also brings destruction and blight.
It reminds us of the duality of existence,
The balance between resistance and persistence
For as we play with fire, we must be aware
Of the consequences, the risks we dare.
But fire also brings passion and drive,
A force that can inspire us to strive
For without the heat of desire,
We would be forever in a state of mire.
So let us harness the fire's energy,
But also learn to control its fury
For in its light, we can see the path to our dreams,
But in its destruction, we see the result of our schemes.
Fire, a force of nature and of mind,
A reminder of the balance we must find
For in its beauty and its devastation,
Lies a lesson, a call to contemplation.
So let us be mindful of the fire we ignite,
For it is the key to our growth and our plight.
For in its light, we can see the path to our evolution,
But in its destruction, we see the result of our revolution.
And as the fire burns and the ashes cool,
We are left with a sense of both wonder and fool
For fire, though it may bring warmth and light,
Also brings destruction and blight.
It reminds us of the cyclical nature of life,
The balance between birth and strife
For as we play with fire, we must be aware
Of the consequences, the choices we share.
But fire also brings transformation and change,
A force that can help us to rearrange

For without the heat of metamorphosis,

We would be forever in a state of stasis.

So let us utilize the fire's power,

But also learn to respect its hour

For in its light, we can see the path to our progress,

But in its destruction, we see the result of our excess.

Fire, a force of nature and of human spirit,

A reminder of the balance we must inherit

For in its beauty and its devastation,

Lies a lesson, a call to integration.

So let us be mindful of the fire we ignite,

For it is the key to our potential and our plight.

For in its light, we can see the path to our enlightenment,

But in its destruction, we see the result of our lament.

And as the fire burns and the ash settles,

We are left with a newfound understanding of the mettle

For fire, though it may bring warmth and light,

Also brings destruction and blight.

It reminds us of the intricacies of existence,

The balance between light and persistence

For as we play with fire, we must be aware

Of the consequences, the actions we share.

But fire also brings creativity and art,

A force that can inspire us to take part

For without the heat of imagination,

We would be forever in a state of stagnation.

So let us use the fire's energy,

But also learn to control its intensity

For in its light, we can see the path to our innovation,

But in its destruction, we see the result of our deviation.

Fire, a force of nature and of human expression,

A reminder of the balance we must possess

For in its beauty and its devastation,

Lies a lesson, a call to introspection.

So let us be mindful of the fire we ignite,

For it is the key to our destiny and our plight.

For in its light, we can see the path to our realization,

But in its destruction, we see the result of our realization.

And as the fire burns and the smoke dissipates,

We are left with a deeper understanding of our fates

For fire, though it may bring warmth and light,

Also brings destruction and blight.

It reminds us of the complexities of life,

The balance between light and strife

For as we play with fire, we must be aware

Of the consequences, the choices we bear.

But fire also brings progress and development,

A force that can help us to reinvent

For without the heat of advancement,

We would be forever in a state of permanence.

So let us harness the fire's power,

But also learn to respect its hour

For in its light, we can see the path to our evolution,

But in its destruction, we see the result of our revolution.

Fire, a force of nature and of human advancement,

A reminder of the balance we must enhance

For in its beauty and its devastation,

Lies a lesson, a call to self-evaluation.

So let us be mindful of the fire we ignite,

For it is the key to our growth and our plight.

For in its light, we can see the path to our enlightenment,

But in its destruction, we see the result of our lamentation.

And as the fire burns and the ashes scatter,

We are left with a heightened sense of matter

For fire, though it may bring warmth and light,

Also brings destruction and blight.

It reminds us of the interconnectedness of all things,

The balance between light and suffering

For as we play with fire, we must be aware

Of the consequences, the impact we share.

But fire also brings hope and resilience,

A force that can help us to transcendence

For without the heat of determination,

We would be forever in a state of stagnation.

So let us use the fire's energy,

But also learn to control its intensity

For in its light, we can see the path to our salvation,

But in its destruction, we see the result of our damnation.

Fire, a force of nature and of human spirit,

A reminder of the balance we must inherit

For in its beauty and its devastation,

Lies a lesson, a call to self-discovery.

So let us be mindful of the fire we ignite,

For it is the key to our potential and our plight.

For in its light, we can see the path to our self-realization,

But in its destruction, we see the result of our self-destruction.

And as the fire burns and the embers fade,

We are left with a sense of both awe and shade.

For fire, though it may bring warmth and light,

Also brings destruction and blight.

It reminds us of the impermanence of all things,

The balance between life and death's rings

For as we play with fire, we must be aware

Of the consequences, the end result we share.
But fire also brings purification and cleansing,
A force that can help us to start anew, releasing
For without the heat of transformation,
We would be forever in a state of stagnation.
So let us harness the fire's power,
But also learn to respect its hour
For in its light, we can see the path to our rejuvenation,
But in its destruction, we see the result of our desolation.
Fire, a force of nature and of human spirit,
A reminder of the balance we must inherit
For in its beauty and its devastation,
Lies a lesson, a call to self-reflection.
So let us be mindful of the fire we ignite,
For it is the key to our growth and our plight.
For in its light, we can see the path to our self-improvement,
But in its destruction, we see the result of our self-movement.

My Dear Reader

Thank You

Note

As I, a breviloquent raptor, wield A lever, with naught else to my design, I generate tones for the aural field In this prosaic orb we call mankind. My actions, though, are but a small part Of forces far beyond my control, For nature holds the key to each chart And sets the laws that govern the whole. But still, I am compelled to explore The workings of this vast machinery, To seek the truth that lies at core And find the answers to humanity. Though some may call it quest I'll seek the truth, with no time to rest.

About The Author .

"Mawphniang, Napoleon of Syadheh, From Ri Bhoi District in Meghalaya, A soul ever-striving, ne'er at ease, With boundless curiosity and verve. He embraces new ideas with open mind, And ventures boldly into unknown lands, Passionately seeking all that life may find, And making use of time's fleeting sands. His inquisitive nature knows no bounds, As he seeks answers to life's enigmas, Though not pretending to have all profound, He simply lives, without life's drama. He cherishes the small things in this sphere, And on a journey of self-discovery, He writes his story, never to fear, Making most of life, ever-unfurled."

P.C : Clarissa Candace Giri